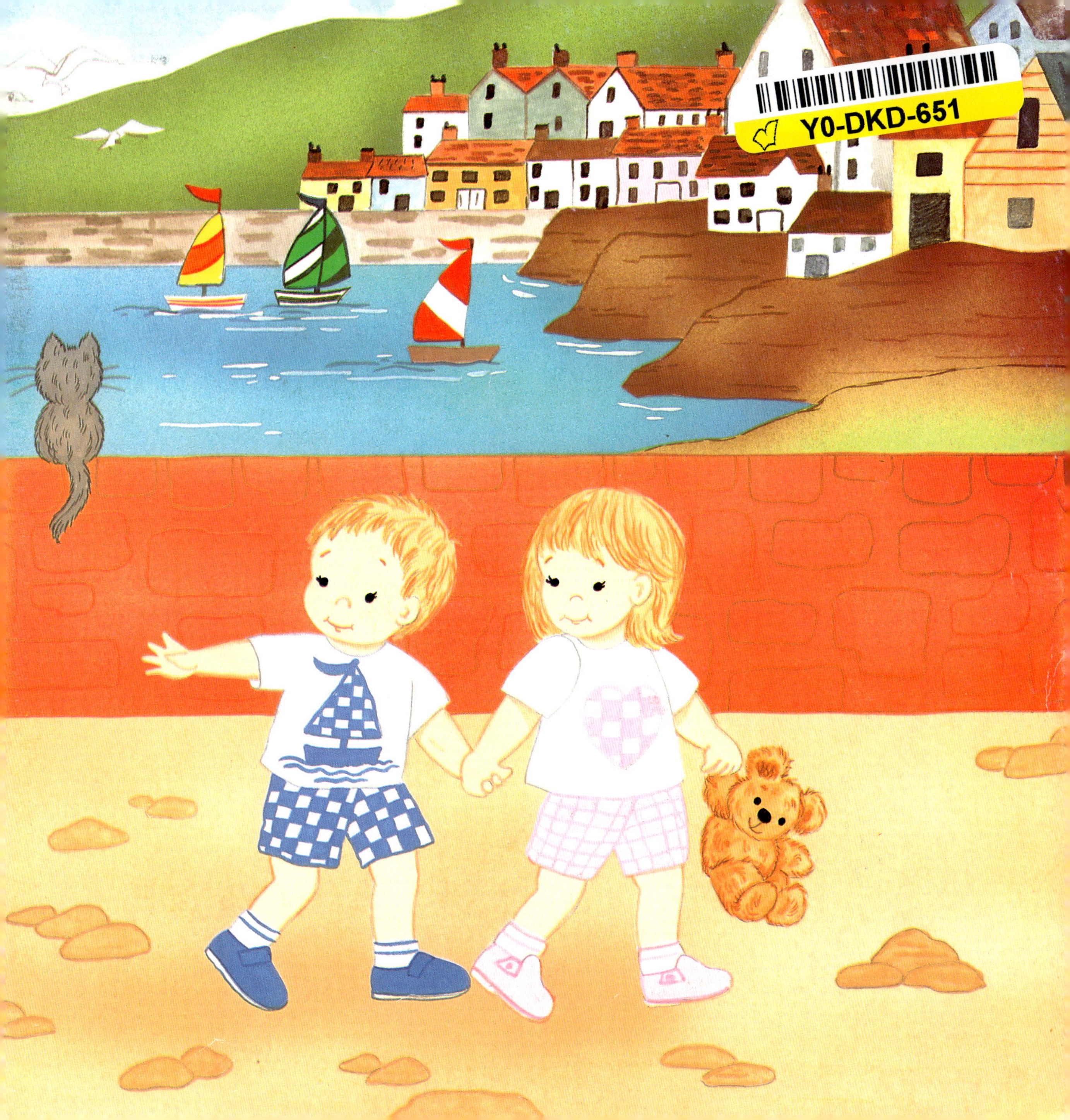

ISBN 1 85854 366 5
© Brimax Books Ltd 1996. All rights reserved.
Published by Brimax Books Ltd, Newmarket,
CB8 7AU, England 1996.
Printed in France - n°67820-A

Going Out

by Gill Davies
Illustrated by Stephanie Longfoot

BRIMAX • NEWMARKET • ENGLAND

It is fun to go outside
And run around and play.

Mother says, "Wear gloves and hats. It's cold outside today."

We like to go for walks.
We can hop and skip and jump.

When we push the buggy fast
The baby laughs at every bump.

Sometimes Father suggests, "Shall we all go to the park?"

Then we take the dog as well,
He loves to run around and bark.

My brother likes the merry-go-round.
I prefer the slide.

There are lots of swings to play on,
And a big see-saw to ride.

We are happy when we go for walks
Across the bridge and by the lake.

We feed the ducks with lots of bread.
What a noise they make!

Each week we go out shopping,
And buy lots of food to eat.

I fill bags with shiny apples,
And grapes that taste so sweet.

The big stores are in the town,
So we drive there in the car.

The toy store is exciting –
It's where the teddy bears are.

It is fun to visit Grandma;
She gives us hugs and lots of fuss.

She shows us photographs of Mother
When she was small like us.

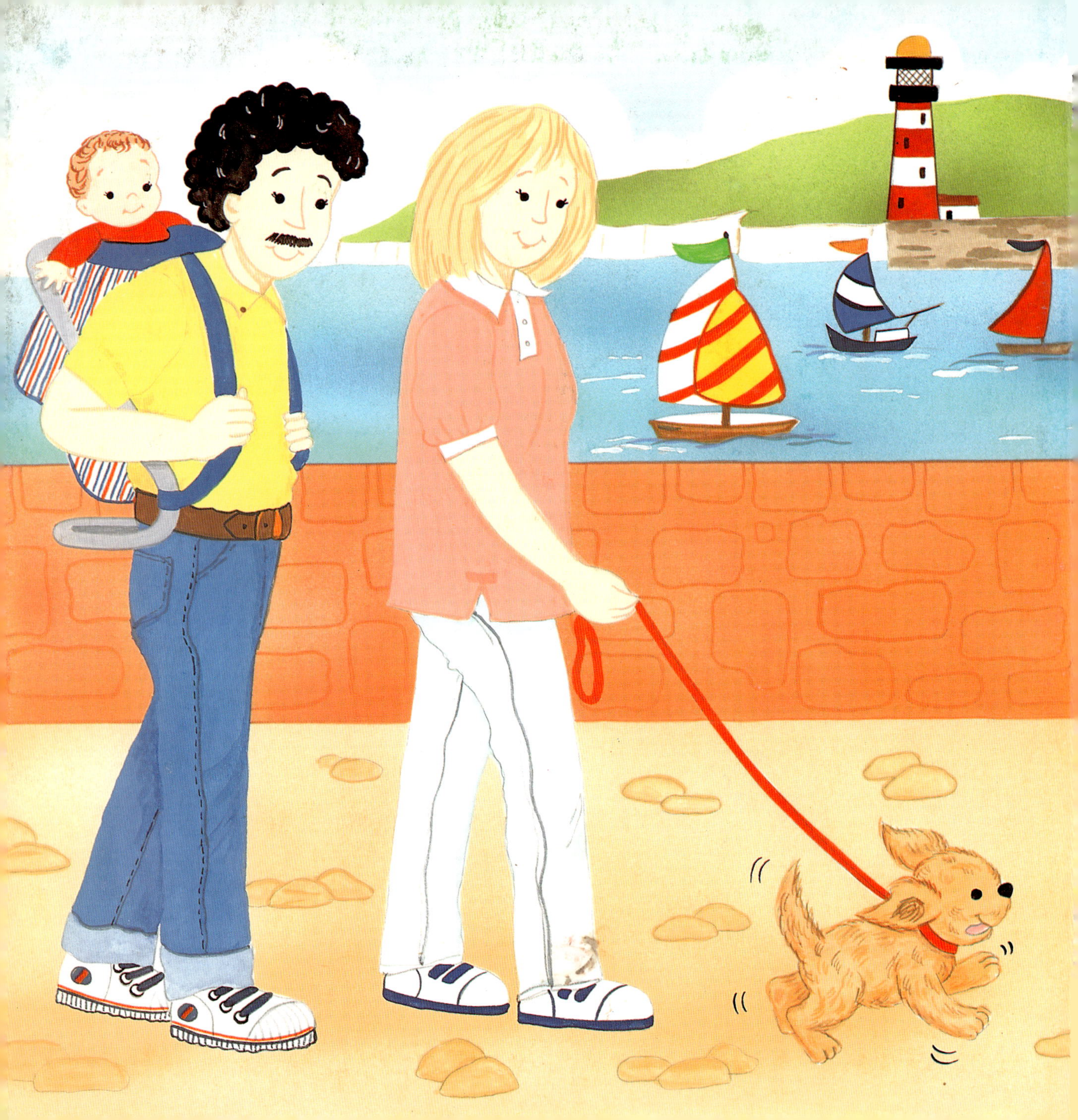